Presented to

_____

On the Occasion of

_____

From

_____

Date

_____

ISBN 1-58660-087-7

All Scripture quotations, unless otherwise noted, are taken from the King James Version of the Bible.

Scripture quotations marked NIV are taken from the HOLY BIBLE: NEW INTERNATIONAL VERSION ®. NIV ®. Copyright © 1973, 1978, 1984 by International Bible Society. Used by permission of Zondervan Publishing House. All rights reserved.

Published by Barbour Publishing, Inc., P.O. Box 719, Uhrichsville, Ohio 44683
www.barbourbooks.com

Member of the
Evangelical Christian
Publishers Association

Printed in China.

The WORD ON LOVE

A BIBLICAL CELEBRATION OF LOVE

BARBOUR
PUBLISHING, INC.

And now these three remain:
faith, hope and love.
But the greatest of these is love.

1 Corinthians 13:13 NIV

Introduction

That first kiss. A romantic candlelight dinner. Vows recited before family and friends. Each memory, and thousands of others like them, are forever locked in our hearts—and create for us a picture of love. Who can deny the power of romantic attraction?

But true love actually travels much deeper than that. It's the long-term commitment, the deliberate act of the will, that keeps a couple together for thirty, forty, or sixty years—or more. The kind of relationship that weathers all storms. The kind of relationship that God intended for marriage.

Since, as the apostle John said, God *is* love, He knows what love is all about. . .and He gave us a picture of love in its purest form in His Son, Jesus Christ. We find a stunning portrait of Him in God's Word, the Bible.

All three kinds of love are beautifully described in the Scriptures, and carefully excerpted in this book. Read on for a fascinating introduction to the world's greatest emotion.

Love is patient, love is kind.
It does not envy,
it does not boast,
it is not proud.
It is not rude,
it is not self-seeking,
it is not easily angered,
it keeps no record of wrongs.
Love does not delight in evil
but rejoices with the truth.
It always protects, always trusts,
always hopes,
always perseveres.
Love never fails.

1 Corinthians 13:4–8 NIV

Romantic Love

Passion is universal humanity.
Without it, religion, history, romance,
and art would be useless.

Honore de Balzac

A relationship generally begins with a spark—
that sometimes grows into a flame. . . .

Behold, thou art fair, my love;
behold, thou art fair; thou hast doves' eyes.
Song of Solomon 1:15

Turn away thine eyes from me,
for they have overcome me.
Song of Solomon 6:5

Set me as a seal upon thine heart,
as a seal upon thine arm: for love is strong as death.
Song of Solomon 8:6

Though romance isn't a main theme of the Bible,
following are two notable examples of romantic attraction:

And the king loved Esther above all the women,
and she obtained grace and favour in his sight more than
all the virgins; so that he set the royal crown upon her head,
and made her queen.
Esther 2:17

And Jacob loved Rachel; and said, I will serve thee seven years
for Rachel thy younger daughter. And Jacob served seven years
for Rachel; and they seemed unto him but a few days,
for the love he had to her.
Genesis 29:18, 20

Here's the romantic story of Ruth and Boaz
at their first face-to-face meeting. . . .

And when Boaz had eaten and drunk, and his heart was merry, he went to lie down at the end of the heap of corn: and she came softly, and uncovered his feet, and laid her down. And it came to pass at midnight, that the man was afraid, and turned himself: and, behold, a woman lay at his feet. And he said, Who art thou? And she answered, I am Ruth thine handmaid: spread therefore thy skirt over thine handmaid; for thou art a near kinsman. And he said, Blessed be thou of the LORD, my daughter: for thou hast shewed more kindness in the latter end than at the beginning, inasmuch as thou followedst not young men, whether poor or rich. And now, my daughter, fear not; I will do to thee all that thou requirest: for all the city of my people doth know that thou art a virtuous woman. And now it is true that I am thy near kinsman: howbeit there is a kinsman nearer than I. Tarry this night, and it shall be in the morning, that if he will perform unto thee the part of a kinsman, well; let him do the kinsman's part: but if he will not do the part of a kinsman to thee, then will I do the part of a kinsman to thee, as the LORD liveth: lie down until the morning.

Ruth 3:7–13

. . .

Let him kiss me with the
kisses of his mouth:
for thy love is
better than wine.

Song of Solomon 1:2

$\mathcal{O}$ perfect Love, all human thought transcending,
Lowly we kneel in prayer before Thy throne,
That theirs may be the love which knows no ending,
Whom Thou forevermore dost join in one.
Grant them the joy which brightens earthly sorrow;
Grant them the peace which calms all earthly strife,
And to life's day the glorious unknown morrow
That dawns upon eternal love and life.
Dorothy Frances Blomfield Gurney, 1883

Marital Love

A successful marriage is an edifice
that must be rebuilt every day.
Andre Maurois

Marriage is, of course, a good thing—because God Himself created it. . . .

Whoso findeth a wife findeth a good thing,
and obtaineth favour of the LORD.
Proverbs 18: 22

And Adam said, This is now bone of my bones, and flesh of my flesh:
she shall be called Woman, because she was taken out of Man.
Genesis 2:23

*Let thy fountain be blessed:
and rejoice with the wife of thy youth.*
Proverbs 5:18

Therefore shall a man leave his father and his mother, and shall
cleave unto his wife: and they shall be one flesh.
Genesis 2:24

The voice that breathed o'er Eden, that earliest wedding day,
The primal wedding blessing, it hath not passed away.
Still in the pure espousal of Christian man and maid
The Triune God is with us, the threefold grace is said.
Be present, loving Father, to give away this bride
As Thou gav'st Eve to Adam, a helpmate at his side.
Be present, Son of Mary, to join their loving hands
As Thou didst bind two natures in Thine eternal bands.
Be present, Holy Spirit, to bless them as they kneel,
As Thou for Christ, the Bridegroom, the heav'nly Spouse dost seal.
Oh, spread Thy pure wing o'er them, let no ill pow'r find place
When onward to Thine altar, their hallowed path they trace.

John Keble, 1857

*Successful, lasting marriages are built on the proper kind of love—the love
that God describes in His Word, the Bible. . . .*

Husbands, love your wives.
Colossians 3:19

Wives, submit to your husbands as to the Lord.
Ephesians 5:22 NIV

Husbands. . .be considerate as you live with your wives,
and treat them with respect.
1 Peter 3:7 NIV

Live joyfully with the wife whom thou lovest all the days of the life. . .
which he hath given thee under the sun. . .for that is thy portion in
this life, and in thy labour which thou takest under the sun.
Ecclesiastes 9:9

This holy vow that man can make,
The golden thread in life,
The bond that none may dare to break,
That bindeth man and wife,
Which, blest by Thee, whate'er betide,
No evil shall destroy,
Through careworn days each care divides
And doubles every joy.
Adelaide Thrupp, 1853

Earthly marriage can serve as a symbol of Christ's
relationship to His church. . . .

For this cause shall a man leave his father and mother, and shall be
joined unto his wife, and they two shall be one flesh. This is a great
mystery: but I speak concerning Christ and the church.
Ephesians 5:31–32

Let us be glad and rejoice, and give honour to him: for the marriage
of the Lamb is come, and his wife hath made herself ready.
And to her was granted that she should be arrayed in fine linen,
clean and white: for the fine linen is the righteousness of saints.
And he saith unto me, Write, Blessed are they which are called unto
the marriage supper of the Lamb. And he saith unto me,
These are the true sayings of God.
Revelation 10:7–9

Lord, Who at Cana's wedding feast
　　Didst as a Guest appear,
Thou dearer far than earthly guest,
　　Vouchsafe Thy presence here.
For holy Thou indeed dost prove
　　The marriage vow to be,
Proclaiming it a type of love
Between the Church and Thee.
Adelaide Thrupp, 1853

God is love; His mercy brightens
All the path in which we rove;
Bliss He wakes, and woe He lightens:
God is wisdom, God is love.
Chance and change are busy ever;
Man decays and ages move;
But His mercy waneth never:
God is wisdom, God is love.
He with earthly cares entwineth
Hope and comfort from above;
Everywhere His glory shineth:
God is wisdom, God is love.

John Bowring, 1825

God's Love

Riches take wings, comforts vanish,
hope withers away, but love stays with us.
God is love.

Lew Wallace

From the dawn of human history,
God has been showing His love to mankind. . . .

And I will establish my covenant between me and thee and thy seed
after thee in their generations for an everlasting covenant, to be a
God unto thee, and to thy seed after thee.

Genesis 17:7

And I will dwell among the children of
Israel, and will be their God.

Exodus 29:45

Ye have seen what I did unto the Egyptians, and how I bare you on
eagles' wings, and brought you unto myself. Now therefore, if ye will
obey my voice indeed, and keep my covenant, then ye shall be a pecu-
liar treasure unto me above all people: for all the earth is mine: And
ye shall be unto me a kingdom of priests, and an holy nation.

Exodus 19:4–6

Behold th'amazing gift of love
The Father hath bestowed
On us, the sinful sons of men,
To call us sons of God!
High is the rank we now possess;
But higher we shall rise;
Though what we shall hereafter be
Is hid from mortal eyes.

Isaac Watts, 1709

The writers of the psalms were intimately acquainted with God's love. . . .

Praise be to the LORD, for he showed his wonderful love to me.
Psalm 31:21 NIV

Yet the LORD will command his lovingkindness in the daytime,
and in the night his song shall be with me,
and my prayer unto the God of my life.
Psalm 42:8

We have thought of thy lovingkindness,
O God, in the midst of thy temple.
Psalm 48:9

Because your love is better than life, my lips will glorify you.
Psalm 63:3 NIV

In heavenly love abiding, no change my heart shall fear.
And safe in such confiding, for nothing changes here.
The storm may roar without me, my heart may low be laid,
But God is round about me, and can I be dismayed?
Wherever He may guide me, no want shall turn me back.
My Shepherd is beside me, and nothing can I lack.
His wisdom ever waking, His sight is never dim.
He knows the way He's taking, and I will walk with Him.
Anna Laetitia Waring, 1850

Here are several more promises of God's love, from the Psalms. . . .

Bless the LORD, O my soul, and forget not all his benefits:
Who forgiveth all thine iniquities; who healeth all thy diseases;
Who redeemeth thy life from destruction; who crowneth thee
with lovingkindness and tender mercies.

Psalm 103:2–4

As a father has compassion on his children,
so the LORD has compassion
on those who fear him.

Psalm 103:13 NIV

The LORD openeth the eyes of the blind: the LORD raiseth them that
are bowed down: the LORD loveth the righteous:

Psalm 146:8

The love of God is greater far than tongue or pen can ever tell;
It goes beyond the highest star, and reaches to the lowest hell;
The guilty pair, bowed down with care, God gave His Son to win;
His erring child He reconciled, and pardoned from his sin.
O love of God, how rich and pure!
How measureless and strong!
It shall forevermore endure
The saints' and angels' song.

Frederick Martin Lehman, 1917

Other Old Testament writers spoke eloquently of God's love. . . .

The way of the wicked is an abomination unto the LORD:
but he loveth him that followeth after righteousness.
Proverbs 15:9

Thou hast in love to my soul delivered it from the pit of corruption:
for thou hast cast all my sins behind thy back.
Isaiah 38:17

The LORD hath appeared of old unto me, saying,
Yea, I have loved thee with an everlasting love:
therefore with lovingkindness have I drawn thee.
Jeremiah 31:3

I have loved you, saith the LORD.
Malachi 1:2

O love of God, how strong and true!
Eternal, and yet ever new;
Uncomprehended and unbought,
Beyond all knowledge and all thought.
O love of God, how deep and great!
Far deeper than man's deepest hate;
Self fed, self kindled, like the light,
Changeless, eternal, infinite.
O heavenly love, how precious still,
In days of weariness and ill,
In nights of pain and helplessness,
To heal, to comfort, and to bless!
Horatius Bonar, 1861

The apostle John recorded several of Jesus' pronouncements
on the love of God. . . .

For God so loved the world, that he gave his only begotten Son,
that whosoever believeth in him should not perish,
but have everlasting life.

John 3:16

He that loveth me shall be loved of my Father,
and I will love him,
and will manifest myself to him.

John 14:21

Jesus answered and said unto him, If a man love me, he will keep my
words: and my Father will love him, and we will come unto him,
and make our abode with him.

John 14:23

Behold, behold the wondrous love,
That ever flows from God above
Through Christ His only Son, Who gave
His precious blood our souls to save.
Behold a fountain in His side,
To all the world is opened wide;
Where all may come, by sin oppressed,
And find in Him sweet peace and rest.
All praise and glory be unto Jesus
For He hath purchased a full salvation;
Behold how wondrous the proclamation,
"Whosoever will may come!"
Frances Jane "Fanny" Crosby,
late nineteenth century

The apostle Paul had much to share regarding God's love. . . .

But God demonstrates his own love for us in this:
While we were still sinners, Christ died for us.
Romans 5:8 NIV

The God of love and peace shall be with you.
2 Corinthians 13:11

But God, who is rich in mercy, for his great love wherewith he loved us, Even when we were dead in sins, hath quickened us together with Christ, (by grace ye are saved;) And hath raised us up together, and made us sit together in heavenly places in Christ Jesus: That in the ages to come he might shew the exceeding riches of his grace in his kindness toward us through Christ Jesus.
Ephesians 2:4–7

Of the themes that men have known,
One supremely stands alone;
Through the ages it has shown,
'Tis His wonderful, wonderful love.
Let the bells of heaven ring,
Let the saints their tribute bring,
Let the world true praises sing
For His wonderful, wonderful love.
Love is the theme, love is supreme;
Sweeter it grows, glory bestows;
Bright as the sun ever it glows!
Love is the theme, eternal theme!
Albert Christopher Fisher, 1913

The book of 1 John is filled with the message of God's love. . . .

Beloved, let us love one another: for love is of God; and every one that loveth is born of God, and knoweth God. He that loveth not knoweth not God; for God is love. In this was manifested the love of God toward us, because that God sent his only begotten Son into the world, that we might live through him. Herein is love, not that we loved God, but that he loved us, and sent his Son to be the propitiation for our sins. Beloved, if God so loved us, we ought also to love one another. No man hath seen God at any time. If we love one another, God dwelleth in us, and his love is perfected in us. Hereby know we that we dwell in him, and he in us, because he hath given us of his Spirit. And we have seen and do testify that the Father sent the Son to be the Saviour of the world. Whosoever shall confess that Jesus is the Son of God, God dwelleth in him, and he in God. And we have known and believed the love that God hath to us. God is love; and he that dwelleth in love dwelleth in God, and God in him.

1 John 4:7–16

Behold, what love, what boundless love,
  The Father hath bestowed
On sinners lost, that we should be
  Now called "the sons of God"!
No longer far from Him but now
  By "precious blood" made nigh,
Accepted in the "Well beloved,"
  Near to God's heart we lie.
  Behold, what manner of love!
What manner of love the Father hath bestowed upon us,
  That we, that we should be called,
  Should be called the sons of God!

Ira D. Sankey,
late nineteenth century

Only a little while, sowing and reaping,
Only a little while, our vigil keeping;
Then we shall gather home, no more to sever,
Clasped in eternal love, blest, blest forever.
Only a little while, heartbreak and sorrow,
Dark though the night may be, cloudless the morrow;
Only a little while, Earth ties to sever,
Then in our Father land, blest, blest forever.
Blest, blest forever,
No more to sever,
Clasped in eternal love,
Blest, blest forever.
Frances Jane "Fanny" Crosby, 1892

Eternal Love

Heaven will be what we have always longed for.
It will be filled with happiness, worship, love. . . .
Billy Graham

God's abundant blessings often benefit all people. But many of the promises found in the Scriptures are only for His own children. If you're not sure that you're a member of God's family, He offers you an incredible invitation.

God would love to adopt you into His family through His Son Jesus Christ. The way to Christ is simple:

1. Admit that you are a sinner. "For all have sinned, and come short of the glory of God." Romans 3:23

2. Believe that Jesus Christ is God the Son Who paid the wages of your sin. "For the wages of sin is death [eternal separation from God]; but the gift of God is eternal life through Jesus Christ our Lord." Romans 6:23

3. Call out to God. "If thou shalt confess with thy mouth the Lord Jesus, and shalt believe in thine heart that God hath raised him from the dead, thou shalt be saved." Romans 10:9